first poems after the stroke

poems by

Shanan Ballam

Finishing Line Press
Georgetown, Kentucky

first poems after the stroke

ACKNOWLEDGMENTS

Sugar House Review: "damage," "facing it," and "april"
Wordgathering: A Journal of Disability Poetry and Literature: "the dream"
Kaleidoscope: "the owls" and "beauty"
Honorable Mention in the Utah Original Writing Competition: "first poem after the stroke," "nobody," "kaleidoscope," "Snapdragons," "the dream," and "damage"

Publisher: Leah Huete de Maines
Editor: Christen Kincaid
Cover Art: Kayla Rich
Author Photo: Brock Dethier
Cover Design: Elizabeth Maines McCleavy

Order online: www.finishinglinepress.com
also available on amazon.com

Author inquiries and mail orders:
Finishing Line Press
PO Box 1626
Georgetown, Kentucky 40324
USA

Contents

first poem after the stroke 1

nobody 2

kaleidoscope 3

Snapdragons 4

the dream 5

damage 7

april 9

the owls 11

impermanence 13

storm warning 16

facing it 18

missing 21

meaning 23

beauty 25

for my husband Brock

first poem after the stroke

    rain of beads dripping
        down alert and determined
    I wake from the fog

        of my life

a scream

    of snow on the branches

of the crabapple tree

        I am a monarch
    butterfly who will emerge
with wet wings jeweled

    with dew, I am a monarch butterfly
with wings jeweled

    and a stained-glass heart

nobody

understands what it is
like to have
a stroke.

knees buck-
      ling and
      the crash

        to the bathroom
    floor

I called out
   to my husband
   for help

      that was the last
thing I said

    for three
     days

kaleidoscope

in the hospital
   I lived inside

      shadows and light
         ever-shifting

         nurses dressed
            in blue

            sifting

   in and out
of my room

      like sand

      I woke
   in a different
      room every day

            furniture
         was moved

   or missing

Snapdragons
--for Brock

You bought
me snapdragons
from the grocery store.
The blossoms
are rust-orange,
but they are emerging
blush pink
and pale yellow
near the top
of the stalk.

I pinch one to see
inside its mouth.
There: three sprigs dusted
with gold pollen,
and the soft toothy trap
designed to rub
pollen off
bumblebees'
legs and feet.

Today is the last
Sunday in February.
I had a massive
stroke on
the 9th of January.

Today I moved
my big toe.

You bought me snapdragons.
You are my hero.

the dream

      the shiny taste
        of rain when I inhale

love leads
    us back to the things
of this world

      the pink roses unfurl
perfume

      the moon is a white lily
          about to bloom

            having a stroke erases half
                the world half

            your working
              body and your

            voice

        the owl in the willow
          is a ghost
        it calls to me through the open
             night window, calls
          to me in my dreams
                in smeared colors

           it sounds
           like windchimes

my lips taste like lilies—

      the cold scent of rain on stones—

    a dark curtain embroidered
                with light

the owl is a prophetess
        singing to me in my sleep

the owl is a part of the willow tree
        is a part of my heart
whispering
        you will recover

fragrance of lilies in a glass vase

the crabapple tree is dotted
        with pearls of rain

my lips taste like water
that is: they have no taste

the rain has turned to snow
        it floats down in swirling spirals
        like falling
                into a dream

the windchime speaks
        in the voice of god
like a waterfall,
                fluid,

like the song
        of a canyon wren
tumbling down
        the canyon

last night I dreamed

I could walk again

damage

the oxygen
deprivation
blossomed
in the brain

It was almost
beautiful
if it hadn't been
my brain

my right
foot
is numb, cold
and heavy
as an anvil

I crashed
to the tile floor

the blue
and black
bruise throbbed
on my thigh

this is my life
trial

I claw
my way through
the cobwebs
of aphasia

dull and empty
my brain

snow on
the crabapple branches
again

I'm radiant
with patience

I will
not break

april

the willow tree is tangled
with sunlight

peace comes dropping
slow

a waterfall
of pink blossoms
outside the window

the lily of the valley glow
like pearls
I wore a spray
in my hair
on my wedding day

fragrant like a rainbow
trembling

four and a half months since
I had the stroke

to know darkness
you must travel
through darkness

its dense forests
of pain

the light is tangled
in my hair

on my eyelashes

bright as feathers

a single sandhill crane
standing in dry lake

like a prophet

I am no stranger to pain

I am afraid to feel

this suffering
is smothering
me like a rag
stuffed
in my mouth

toss my losses
into the river's green
gloss

I see a horse
a chestnut horse
munching meadow grass
it approaches me
comes closer
and my grief
dissolves

a single red leaf
dotted with dew
turns
on still water

the owls

        in the nest
we spot them:

    two baby
great horned owls,
      fluffy
        and camouflaged

     to look like
decaying
tree matter

     huge eyes, flecked
        with gold shimmer,
      stare out at us

      a pink
crabapple petal,
   thin as tissue
     paper,
       clings
to my walker

     loosen
your grip

      on helplessness
and sorrow

       the crocus petals
        are dusted
with saffron

a wash of light
on the ash tree

the gold
light shining
in the owls' eyes

impermanence

the ditch flows
forget-me-nots
sway
underwater

blue and blurry
drowning eyes

I dose myself until
I become a ghost

abyss of bliss

I'm lost

in silence

I have vaguely
considered
suicide

a bird sings
in the distance
in some far tree

a single white butterfly
dips
and flutters

flutters and dips
a single white
butterfly

it's getting dimmer
        the light
    falls
        slow

        I hold
    to the hope
that I'll be able
        to walk
by the end
        of the summer

                a few birds stain
            the sky

            last night
        the skunk's dark
                fragrance
        wafted in the open
                window

            sunlight goldens
                the silky grass

        a single white
            feather clings
                    to the columbine

        one buttercup
            remains
                on the path

                wild roses near
            the river
        the petals of the last
                living
        rose drifted off

sometime over
night

ephemeral
this world
and the things

in it

a single
sandpiper perches
on the stick
in the middle
of the river

it appears
every day

I wonder when
it will

disappear

storm warning

lightning
      to the south
   big daggers
         flash

low moan
   of frogs

a pair of eagles
    deliberate
     slow
    flapping

    mosquitos
  feed on us

wind ruffling
   the willow tendrils

sloppy
  hopping

   a leopard frog

indian paintbrush
   glowed
 red
   candles
  in the marsh

and the wild
   cucumber
 cascades
   of cream blossoms

three
   sandhill cranes alighted

in the far
field

little white flowers
blooming
in the water

yesterday I talked
on the phone
to my sister

when she told me
she was going
to hike katahdin
in September

I cried

she was certain
I will make a full
recovery and we would
hike katahdin
together

lavender crush
lush river
rush
of grass-
hopper
wings

two monarch
caterpillars munch
on milkweed
getting plump

from the stream
a night heron rises

facing it

I've lost
  the ability
    to walk

I can't do
  stairs
  or go
    uphill
    or downhill

I've lost
  my beautiful
penmanship

    but I can let go
  of things with
    my right hand
I used to grip
  so hard
    the handrail
    in rehab—

I've relearned
  how to use
    chopsticks

I can open
  pill bottles
    and La Croix cans

I haven't lost
  the ability to
write poetry

    I made it up
  and down
    little mountain

cascades
of birdsong and then
silence

graceful arcs
silver spray
of sprinklers
in the far field

three sandhill cranes
flying in unison
three sandhill cranes
dissolved
into the mountain

a skunk plumes
its luxurious
black and white
tail

a deer bounding

a monarch
butterfly
up close
for the first
time

flashing its wings
opening and
closing
its wings

perched
on an elm leaf
mesmerizing
near the river

perched on an elm leaf
opening
and closing
its wings
near
the river

opening
and closing

missing

the moon is close
　　to being full again

today is the nine-month

anniversary

　　of my stroke

I'm still struggling

　　to walk

further in the wetlands
　　than
we have
　　　ever gone

open water

a waterfall

　　of birdsong

then silence

a wash of light
　　pale yellow

on the foothills

　　almost white

we haven't seen
　　the great
blue heron in weeks

or the kingfisher
who perches
above the scuzzy pond

I'm concerned
that the feeling
in my right foot
won't return

the russian sage
is finally blooming
a spray of fuzzy
purple blossoms

a secret patch
of yellow aspen
glows
on the high
slope

meaning

catching
my eye
black and orange
flutter
a monarch
butterfly

graceful willow
branches arch
across the river

I can still see
the ducks
receding

the sun was about
to set when we saw
the moon
full and rising
above
foothills washed
in rose light

the river's
brown-green glint

bees crowd
the milkweed
blossoms

whir of wings

I long to feel

rainbow stretching
across the sky

the bluebirds
were another sign
of luck

a painted lady
landed
on my hand
and stayed there

lovely
the grasses
rippling
in the wind

only once I lost
my balance

life has meaning
but I wonder

a great blue heron
glides
across
an orange sunset

a single
pink orchid
trembles
in pine duff

magenta
with a spotted
tongue

the fairy
slipper orchid

I have been
searching
for all my life

beauty

a slate-blue

dipper
in the logan river

dipping
on thin legs

in the wetlands
silver strands

of spider silk draped
across the road

all at once and
spontaneously

spinning out silk

floating

endlessly

two colts
one all black

a white star

on its forehead

one chestnut brown
with all white feet

followed me along
the fence
nudging
its velvet nose

           three sandhill
cranes

        sailing

            across
a dusk-blue sky

a monarch butterfly
  on the path

motionless

       dark orange
         black outlines

  that look like

         they were drawn

    by a felt tip pen

         ink bleeding

    delicate

            antennae

       legs

  white spots on the body
     and wings

we thought it was dead

    but in the car

      it started to move

        unfolding its wings

    when we got home

      I laid it in the milkweed

        breathing

Shanan Ballam is a Senior Lecturer at Utah State University where she teaches poetry writing and composition. She survived a massive stroke in January 2022 which left her without speech and without the use of the entire right side of her body. She never quit writing poetry, though, and she was awarded an Honorable Mention in the Utah Original Writing Contest for her entry "first poems after the stroke" in October of 2022. She has published one chapbook, *The Red Riding Hood Papers* (Finishing Line 2010) and two full-length poetry manuscripts, *Pretty Marrow* (Negative Capability 2013) and *Inside the Animal: The Collected Red Riding Hood Poems* (Main Street Rag 2019), a semi-finalist for the 2017 Trio House Press Louise Bogan Award and a finalist for the 2017 Hillary Gravendyk Prize Poetry Book Competition from Inlandia Press. She was a 2022 finalist for the James Hearst Poetry Award. Her work has recently appeared in *North American Review, Plume, I-70 Review, Wordgathering: A Journal of Disability Poetry and Literature, Kaleidoscope* and *Sugar House Review*.

www.ingramcontent.com/pod-product-compliance
Lightning Source LLC
Chambersburg PA
CBHW022058080426
42734CB00009B/1398